SHIKSHA

SHIKSHA
A JOURNEY TO CONQUER EDUCATION

Aishwarya Krishnan

Notion Press

Old No. 38, New No. 6
McNichols Road, Chetpet
Chennai – 600 031

First Published by Notion Press 2017
Copyright © Aishwarya Krishnan 2017
All Rights Reserved.

ISBN 978-1-948321-45-7

"Education is not just for a privileged few, it is for everyone. It is a fundamental human right ."

Ban Ki-moon

VILLAGE IN A RURAL AREA OF KOLKATA

KAMALA HURRY UP! WE NEED TO LEAVE.

I'M COMING, MA.

CHATTER
CHATTER
CHATTER

THIS IS KAMALA, A 13-YEAR-OLD GIRL WHO LIVES IN A VILLAGE IN KOLKATA.

A FEW DAYS AGO, SHE WAS FORCED TO QUIT SCHOOL DUE TO SOME HOUSEHOLD CIRCUMSTANCES.
PLEASE MA!
I REALLY WANT TO GO!

HOW DARE YOU ASK ME SUCH A QUESTION!
YOU KNOW WE NEED MORE MONEY!

YOU KNOW VERY WELL THAT WE AREN'T
SOME RICH, HIGH-CLASS FAMILY.
GOING TO SCHOOL IS NOT OF CONCERN TO US.

EDUCATION IS NOT
AS IMPORTANT AS
EARNING MONEY!
FROM ... ROW
YOU ... K AS A
CO... AY A ROLE
IN ... R FATHER MONEY!
A... ...T YOU WILL GET MARRIED
TO... OF THE SAME CAST AS
... GIVE ... THE BLESSING
... SONS INTO
... IMPORTANT THAT
... A COOK, IN OUR
...DUCATIO... LEAST
...ANCE. YO... WANTS YOU
... A HIGH S... ROM A HOUSE
..., TOMOR... WILL COME W
... TOGETH... LL GET YOU A
...WORK A... OUSEHOLD THE
...ILL PRO... ORE MONEY.
...OP CRY... IT WONT SO
...HING, YO... REALIZE TH...
... HUSBA... BE WORKING
... DO NOT ...RGE... RING IN MANY

...AND HERE SHE IS NOW.

YES, YES! SHE COOKS VERY WELL!
HMM... SHE SEEMS LIKE A DILIGENT GIRL.
WELL THEN! FOR LUNCH I WANT YOU TO MAKE RAJMA CHAWAL, ALOO GOBI ...

THE KITCHEN IS THAT WAY.

ARE YOU LISTENING?

YES.
GOOD, THEN GET TO WORK.

KAMALA LOVES TO WRITE WHENEVER SHE FINDS THE TIME. AFTER A LONG DAY OF WORK, KAMALA SITS IN A CORNER OF THE KITCHEN AND WRITES TO HER HEARTS CONTENT.

THE LADY OF THE HOUSE WAS CURIOUS AND ASKED WHAT KAMALA WAS WRITING. KAMALA THEN SHOWED IT TO HER.

MY FAMILY DOESN'T REALLY CONSIDER IT IMPORTANT. AND EITHER WAY, WE DON'T HAVE THE MONEY.
THE LADY OF THE HOUSE KEPT ASKING WHY SHE WOULDN'T GO TO SCHOOL AND THE RESPONSE WAS THE SAME EVERY TIME.

A LITTLE WHILE LATER...
I WANT YOU TO UNDERSTAND THAT SHE IS A YOUNG GIRL. IT IS IMPORTANT FOR HER TO GO TO SCHOOL.

UNFORTUNATELY, KAMALA'S MOTHER WAS NOT PERSUADED AT ALL.

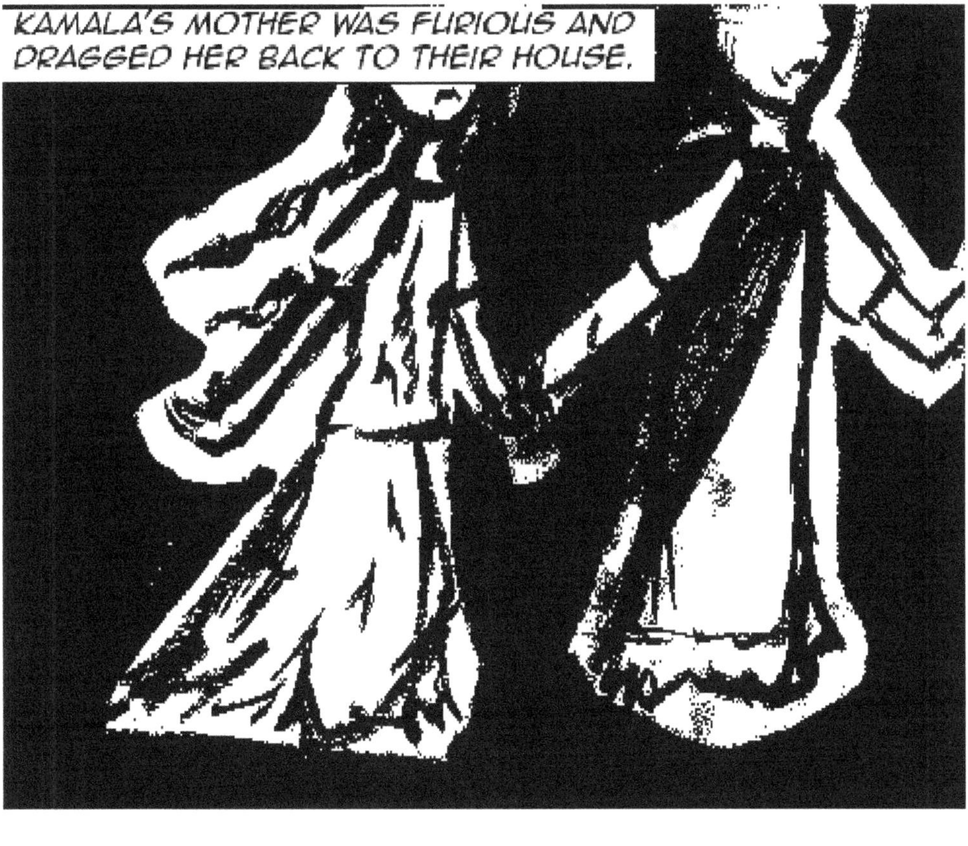

KAMALA'S MOTHER WAS FURIOUS AND DRAGGED HER BACK TO THEIR HOUSE.

I HEARD SOME NONSENSE FROM YOUR MOTHER. I WANT TO KNOW IF ANY OF IT IS TRUE.

YOU KNOW THAT EDUCATION ISN'T IMPORTANT. HOW DARE YOU COMPLAIN AT YOUR WORKPLACE. KNOW YOUR POSITION!

IF YOU DARE TRY AND ACT SMART I WILL NEVER LET YOU GO THERE AGAIN!

KAMALA WAS SHAKEN UP BY THOSE WORDS, BUT AT THE SAME WAS ANGERED BY THEM.

FATHER. MADAM SAID THAT I MUST GO TO SCHOOL. SHE WAS IMPRESSED BY MY WRITING SKILLS. FATHER I WANT TO BE EDUCATED!

13

I WANT TO KEEP WRITING AND PURSUE IT AS MY CAREER.
HER FATHER WAS SHOCKED AND ASKED TO SEE SOME WORKS SHE HAD PREVIOUSLY WRITTEN.

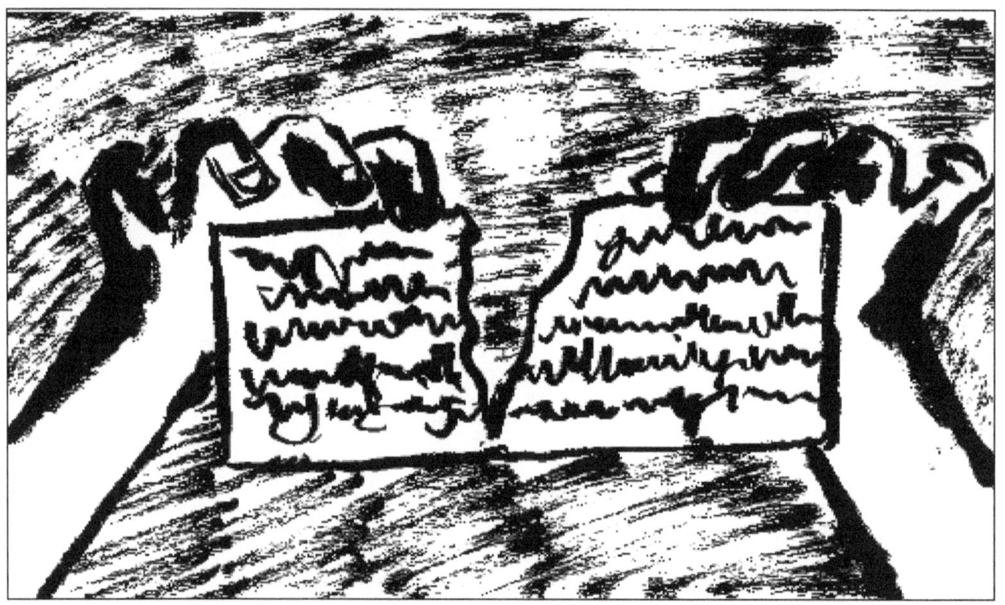

KAMALA HAD NOT EXPECTED HER FATHER TO TEAR UP HER WORK OUT OF ANGER. ALL HER HOPES SUDDENLY SEEMED TO VANISH.

THE FOLLOWING DAY, HER FATHER PROHIBITED HER FROM CONTINUING TO WORK AS A COOK.

DING DONG

THE FATHER TOOK HIS FAMILY TO THE LADY'S HOUSE TO MAKE SURE SHE DOESN'T INTERFERE IN THEIR MATTERS EVER AGAIN.

THE LADY OF THE HOUSE WAS EXTREMELY SURPRISED BY THEIR VISIT.

PLEASE SEND YOUR DAUGHTER TO SCHOOL. SHE IS YOUNG AND DESERVES TO BE EDUCATED.

IF YOU WANT, I CAN HELP BY PAYING ALL OF HER SCHOOL EXPENSES.

HOW DARE YOU MEDDLE WITH OUR ISSUES! OUR CAST AND FAMILY DO NOT HAVE THE TIME FOR EDUCATION!
KAMALA'S FAMILY WENT BACK HOME, ANGRY OVER ALL THE PROBLEMS CAUSED IN THE PAST FEW DAYS.

HE DECIDED TO LET HER CONTINUE WORKING AT THE LADY'S HOUSE.

MEANWHILE, THE LADY OF THE HOUSE WAS HOSTING HER WEEKLY TEA PARTIES.

LADIES I HAVE A PROBLEM! THE COOK AT MY HOUSE IS A YOUNG CHILD! SHOULDN'T SHE BE IN SCHOOL?

OH SO SHE'S THE NEW GIRL?
SHE DEFINITELY DOES LOOK VERY YOUNG!
SHE COOKS WELL!
SHE SEEMS VERY QUIET.
LAUGHTER

IF THESE KIDS START GOING TO SCHOOL, THEN WHO WILL WORK FOR ALL OF US?

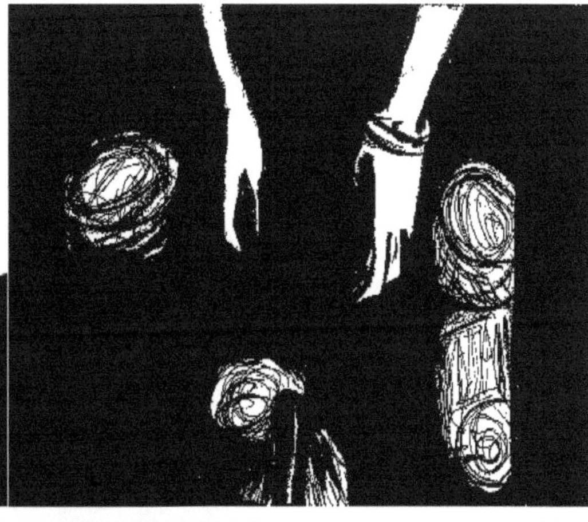

AFTER THE PARTY, THE LADY OF THE HOUSE CALLED KAMALA'S MOTHER TO DISCUSS THE ISSUE OF KAMALA'S EDUCATION.

I WILL SEND KAMALA TO SCHOOL AND PAY FOR ALL HER EXPENSES.

KAMALA AND HER MOTHER GLADLY ACCEPTED THE OFFER. KAMALA TOOK THE LADY'S BLESSINGS.

5 6 7 8 9 10 11 12

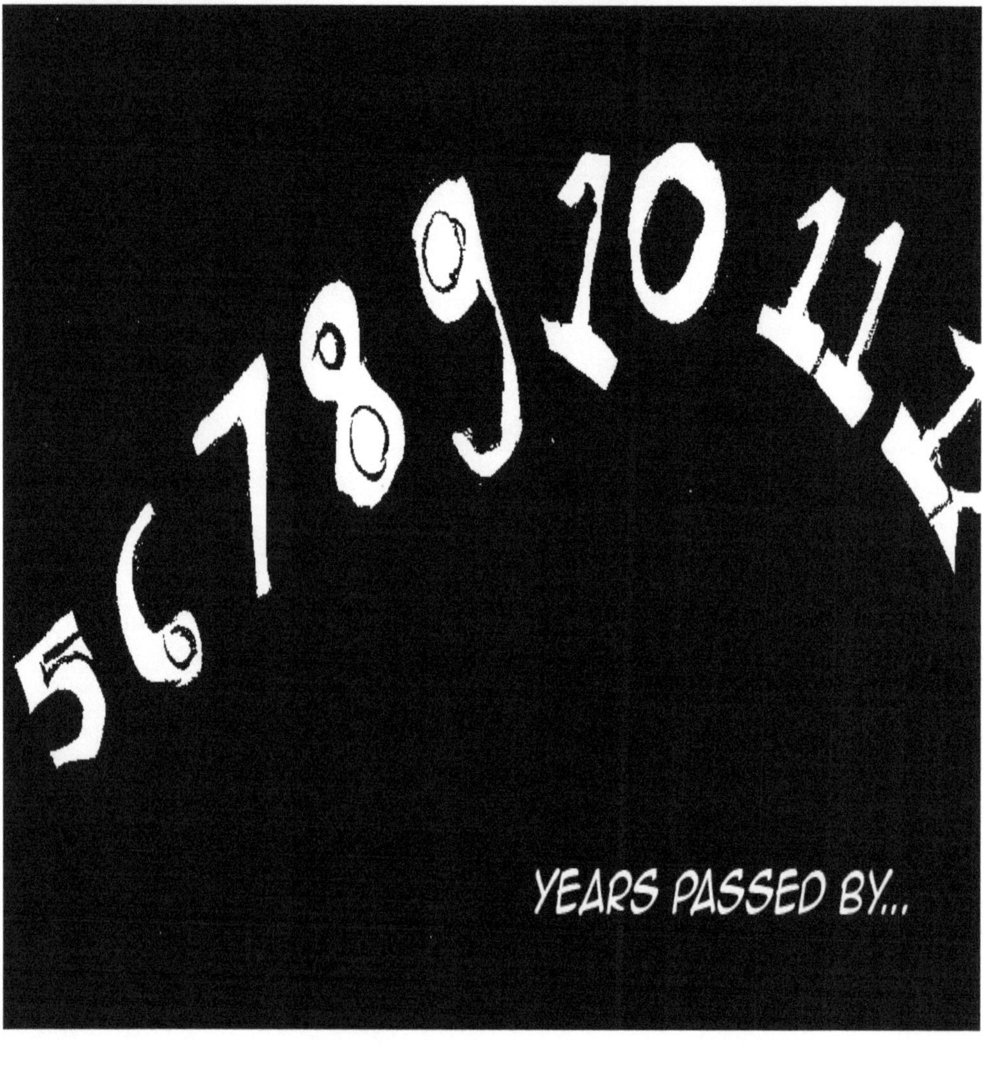

YEARS PASSED BY...

KAMALA GRADUATED...
SHE ACHIEVED A LOT.
WINNER

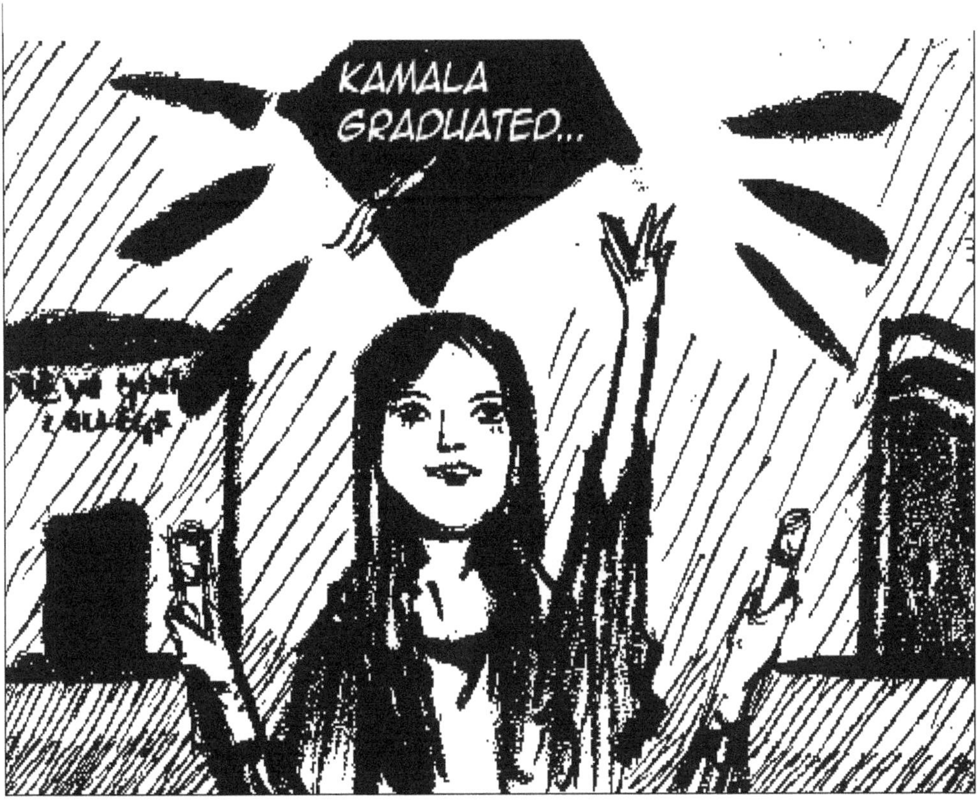

THE LADY WHOSE HOUSE KAMALA USED TO WORK IN, KEPT SUPPORTING KAMALA AND HER DREAMS.

KAMALA APPLIED FOR THE POSITION OF A TEACHER IN A GOVERNMENT SCHOOL.

... SHE GOT THE JOB ...

Adjectives
Pretty
Bland
Spicy
Sweet
SHE WAS A WONDERFUL TEACHER AND HER STUDENTS LOVED HER

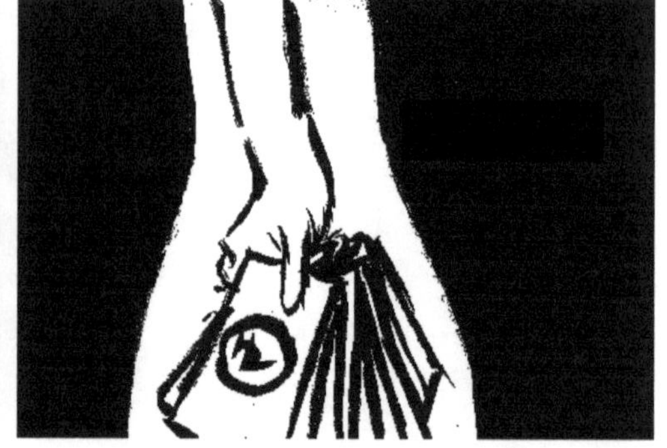

SHE FINALLY HAD ENOUGH MONEY TO BUILD HER DREAM CASTLE.

EDUCATION TODAY WILL PREPARE ONE FOR TOMORROW'S FUTURE.

ALL CHILDREN SHOULD AND MUST HAVE THE RIGHT TO BASIC EDUCATION .... UNFORTUNATELY VERY OFTEN DENIED BY SOCIAL, ECONOMIC AND OTHER PERSONAL CIRCUMSTANCES.

SHIKSHA SCHOOL
LET NO CHILD BE LEFT BEHIND!